Leading Beyond Now

Five Commitments for Africa to Thrive

Ethel Kuuya

LEADING BEYOND NOW

For my children

Thank you for shaping my understanding of a worthy custodian; for showing me how my influence is shaping you and for shaping me with yours. Thank you for the wisdom of your untarnished words and curious questions. Thank you for showing me what it is to be less grown up and more 'growed down'.

Thank you, my souls, for leading me beyond myself.

To Sinqobile.

I wish we'd had more time with you.

I wish you had had the chance to make your dreams come true.

Rest in peace my friend.

CONTENTS

iv

LEADING BEYOND NOW

Preface

Here we are, the current occupants of a property with stress cracks and bowed walls and fissures built into the foundation. We are the heirs to whatever is right or wrong with it. We did not erect the uneven pillars or joists, but they are ours to deal with now. Any further deterioration is, in fact, on our hands.

- Isabel Wilkerson, Caste: the Origins of our Discontents

common thread unites us all across these African nations that are marked by distinct histories, languages, and cultures – it is the aspiration for leadership that genuinely nurtures, uplifts, and endures. This book, *Leading Beyond Now: Five Commitments for Africa to Thrive*, endeavours to distil the essence of such leadership, offering a beacon of wisdom to guide the way.

Over the course of two decades working in corporate strategy, leadership, transformation and research in Africa and internationally, I have collaborated with, advised and coached leaders across sectors. I have had the opportunity to be awestruck and inspired, but also dumb-founded and disappointed. What I have finally put down in this book has been lodged in my throat and languishing in my heart for several years, shaping and morphing until both the time and the message found each other on these pages.

I contemplated the manner to present this message - a large volume of case studies and academic arguments - or, a concise presentation of a simple humanity-based philosophy that is easily recognisable and relatively applicable by anyone. I chose the latter. I was still presented with a challenge – demonstrate the Five Commitments through examples that chronicle rot and poverty throughout Africa or, through examples that elevate and reinforce, more of who we are and can be. Again, I chose the latter.

Such is the gravity of what we, as Africans, need to do, that it cannot be hidden in over-intellectualised verbose volumes. I hope that the tenets proposed in this book become a fulcrum for how we show up as Africans.

It's Not a Country, I Know

Africa is not a monolith; its nations are intricate mosaics, each one radiating its own unique hues and stories. Within this kaleidoscope, my intention is not to homogenise or dictate. Instead, it is a resounding call – a rallying cry - for unity through shared principles. In recognising that diversity *is* our strength, this book seeks to underline that, regardless of the miles that separate us, the heartbeat of responsible leadership must resonate in a common rhythm across the deserts, plains and forests of this continent.

On Brevity

This work is intentionally concise. The truth is, profound commitments need not be verbose or labyrinthine; they can emerge from simplicity, clarity, and genuine intention. In the noise of all the responsibilities that besiege leaders, this book offers a moment of quiet reflection, inviting leaders to recalibrate their compasses and engage in self-assessment.

Ethos

The core philosophy hinges on a timeless concept: that leadership is a torch passed from hand to hand, each bearer illuminating the path for the next. It echoes through history, from the wisdom of ancient elders beneath the African stars to the vibrant energy of modern cities. It is the foundation upon which prosperous societies are built – a philosophy that propels nations forward with an unwavering sense of purpose.

Yet, we have somehow disfigured leadership into the battle of the blood thirsty, where stamina is derived from the depths we sink to and not the heights we can rise to. We are in a woefully dangerous place, where acting from integrity is seen as weakness and corruption is rewarded.

On Thinking Critically

The 'led' must remember that what will save us is critical thinking and decisive action. We are not helpless and feeble people whose destiny it is to be relegated to cowering and whispering dissent while those who steal, and plunder boisterously dominate all spheres of society.
We must think critically, and this involves questioning, analysing, and considering multiple perspectives.

It is a cause of life and death to gather information from diverse sources, remain open to changing your opinion based on new insights, and engage in constructive dialogue when assessing or choosing leaders. At every turn, ask *Why?*

If you fail to think critically and ask questions you are ripe for radicalisation and sycophancy.

In Pursuit of Bold Horizons

Emerging from the ambitious framework of the African Union's Agenda 2063 - The Africa We Want, which encompasses both daring and indispensable strategies, a significant stride has been taken on the continent's transformative path. This progression extends from the pivotal African Continental Free Trade Area (AFCFTA) to the proactive youth initiatives within the SAHEL region.

A distinct departure from the bygone era of liberation-focused politics and entrapped leadership is actively shaping a forward-looking political landscape anchored in sovereignty. Evidently, this journey has commenced with clear intent and purpose.

The essence of my proposition does not stem from a lack of direction. On the contrary, it underscores our well-defined trajectory and comprehension of the continent's imperatives. *It is precisely due to our ambition, awakening to our agency and comprehensive grasp of the continent's necessities, that the call to lead beyond now resonates compellingly.*

The current juncture demands an elevation of our aspirations. Now, more than ever, there exists an imperative to set higher benchmarks and strive for greater achievements.

A Manual for Living

At its heart, this work is a multi-use narrative. It is a roadmap to discern leaders' intentions, insist on accountability, and actively participate in shaping our shared destiny. It is, equally, a handbook for leaders; a mirror held up to reflect our actions against collective aspirations. Whether the leadership role is in the home, at school or a nation, these Five Commitments should serve us.

These principles are based on ancient truths reverberating across time and civilisations. Through integrity, leaders uphold their promises. Through stewardship, they manage resources with care. Through inclusivity, they celebrate the diversity that enriches nations. Through legacy, they sow the seeds for future generations. And, through continuity, they ensure that the journey never halts; immutable facts that are needed now more than at any other time in our history.

My hope for this book is that it may inspire critical conversation in all areas of life where care is required. My hope is that it may spark debate among students, that it finds wear and tear in the palms of activists and, significantly, that it resonates in the hearts of citizens yearning for a brighter future. Leadership is not a solitary endeavour but a symphony of voices, a convergence of minds, and a testament to the audacious hope that tomorrow can be infinitely better than today.

Are these commitments a high bar? Idealistic? Possibly. But if we do not aspire for the heady heights of humanity, then what are we doing? Even when leaders fail, are we not better served by those who fail while in pursuit of lofty ideals than those who fail in pursuit of the mediocre?

And so, I invite leaders in Africa who dare to look beyond the immediate horizon and pledge to be not just stewards of office, but guardians of the future. I challenge you to traverse the terrain of leadership. To build upon the strengths of our past to shape a future that transcends borders, limitations; and time itself.

PART ONE

An Urgent Crescendo

Africa's history has borne witness to an era where the distinctive essence of all 54 states are entwined in such profound challenges and, simultaneously, possibilities as vast as the horizon. There is almost no country where people are not restless for change. The atmosphere is thick with a pressing urgency that only the most discerningly impartial can see clearly - a crescendo of challenges demanding us to rethink our roles as citizens, leaders, and allies. The measure of our mettle shall be the legacy our progeny inherits from us.

The continent's demographic dividend and vast resources are pivotally intertwined, forming the foundation of its progression. Paradoxically, this connection reveals both potential and the threat of stagnation. In the crucible where these two forces converge, a storm of tensions and conflicts are intensifying.

Yet, the future remains changeable. As custodians of our shared legacy, we are at a crossroads where the chasm between aspiration and reality calls on us to close it. It is an ardent summons for us to rise, united; to chart a trajectory that diverges from the chapters of history.

Our burgeoning young population can fuel economic growth through strategic investments in education, healthcare, technology, and a purposeful, nation-centric industrial drive. Without drastic policy and implementation overhauls the chance to leverage this demographic advantage may be squandered. The glaring disparity between our resource-rich communities and, pervasive poverty is not just disheartening, it is evidence of sociopathic leadership.

In an era where global connectivity coexists with stark polarisations, leadership within Africa's corporate, political, and social realms holds unprecedented importance.

The African landscape is in flux across political, commercial, societal, and economic spheres. As powerful countries from the West and East compete on the continent, we need to ask: Are we just pawns in their game? Do our leaders grasp the profound shifts required in approach?

The dynamism of adversities like pandemics, geopolitical shifts, resource abundance and scarcity, a burgeoning youth demographic, external influences, and internal tensions, means we should seek leaders resilient in adversity and devoted to dignity and humanity.

Precisely because Africa has born witness to the cracks in young and old democracies alike - polarisation, marginalisation, and historic, glossed-over animosities - it must unearth clear, impactful commitments, especially for those in leadership, to transition from mere survival to sustained success.

As the world careens into an era of unprecedented complexity, the African continent emerges as a stage for unparalleled potential and profound challenges.

A Geopolitical Cauldron

While understanding global geopolitics is crucial for leaders, regardless of the domain or scale of their leadership, it cannot be the overriding determinant for national priorities. Appreciating global dynamics helps inform leaders' ability to navigate the complex web of international relations more effectively. Countries on the continent today are faced with an inexhaustible mix of complex dynamics.

The emergence of multipolarity

The dawn of the 21st century ushered in a multidimensional showcase of power in Africa. While traditional western titans have maintained their presence, the continent has found new partners in nations like China, India, Brazil, and Turkey, weaving a more intricate geopolitical tapestry.

In the grand theatre of geopolitics, China's meteoric rise has been nothing short of dramatic. With the Belt and Road Initiative as its *magnum opus*, China has become a central figure on the African continent, reshaping both economic and political narratives. Leaders should be centrally aware of the risk and short-term benefit of capitulating to the demands of nations pursuing their own nations' interests.

A 'free' shiny skyscraper is not an equal barter for the future of generations to come. Nothing is.

Democracy

It remains elusive at best and unattainable at worst on the continent. The principle of democracy is unassailable and needs to be crafted within the intricacies and sensitivities that serve Africa. The prevailing brand of leadership is wholly un-African. A relentless tug of war between self-installed life presidents and the desperation for economic prosperity, peace, security, and healthcare, has led to a rising occurrence of *coups*.

The shadow of security

Dark clouds in the form of extremist groups have cast their shadows, challenging the continent's quest for peace and stability.

Drive for economic unity

The African Continental Free Trade Area (AfCFTA) is Africa's thrust for economic ambition, promising to choreograph the most extensive free trade market on the global stage. Despite massive strides, the inconsistency of commitment and dedication by various countries is standing in the way of achieving the envisioned goals under the agreement.

Irresistible land

Africa's trove of natural resources continues to be an irresistible lure for global powers. While sometimes igniting the flames of conflict, these resources also hold the key to a renaissance of prosperity if wielded wisely.

Climate calamity

The undeniability of climate change resonates deeply within Africa. Desertification, dwindling waters, and capricious rainfall patterns are rewriting the security narrative, influencing migration sagas and diplomatic relations.

Unceasing health crises

From the relentless scourge of HIV-AIDS to the unpredictable playout of Ebola and COVID-19, Africa's health nightmare underscores the importance of resilience especially as the global West revealed its hand in vaccine racism. Independent and sound health infrastructure should be a priority following the spectacle of access to COVID-19 vaccines.

Rising regional cooperation

Entities like the African Union (AU) and its various organs are finally straightening their spines and raising assertive voices, championing African solutions for African challenges. Increasingly, political leaders are holding each other accountable across regions but the momentum needs to gather and move to swift coordinated action and cooperation.

Digital revolution

The rise of tech start-ups is a testament to Africa's capacity to leapfrog narratives, shaping its economic destiny and sculpting new forms of socio-political expression; *if* strategically and proactively enabled.

The Resurgence of Coups

In the span between 2013 and 2020, the political air bore a semblance of tranquillity. But things have changed, with over a dozen *coup* attempts that have stretched beyond regional boundaries across the continent. Looking further back, however, we see a bigger picture: since 1950 up until mid-2023, around 220 *coups* have happened in Africa, both successful and unsuccessful.

This grim reality illustrates the complex power dynamics that have influenced many nations. Africa's *coup* history is significant, making up 44 per cent of all global *coup* attempts. Sudan has the highest count at 17 *coups*, reflecting its complex power struggles.

Other countries like Burundi, Ghana, and Sierra Leone have also faced multiple *coup* attempts. There is obviously a direct correlation between dictatorship, leaders who will not step aside, economic woes and *coups*.

The more democracy is nurtured, and leaders leave office in good time, the less likely *coups* will become.

In history's grand tapestry, each *coup* is a stroke that paints the picture of power, ambition, and resistance shaping Africa.

These moments leave an indelible mark on the continent's unfolding story.

A Ticking Debt Bomb

Africa's escalating debt is a crisis underway. The continent is grappling with its most daunting debt burden in over a decade, a consequence of centuries of its resources being gouged from the earth, the scourge of pandemics, wars, and the lurking spectre of rampant inflation.

Alarmingly, 21 of Africa's most vulnerable nations are now teetering on the precipice of bankruptcy or are ensnared in the throes of severe debt distress.

The financial turbulence has seen a significant surge in debt service payments over the past decade, predominantly driven by heightened interest demands on private loans. The predictions cast a shadow on the future. By 2024, Africa's external debt service will likely soar to US$74 billion.

As a poignant case, Nigeria is set to earmark 59 per cent of its 2023 revenue for external and domestic debt servicing. This eclipses its health and education budgets combined, with the scale tilted over twice as much in favour of debt.

Perhaps most troublingly, even before the grip of the Covid-19 pandemic, a third of the continent - 32 African nations - channelled more funds into servicing debt than fortifying their healthcare systems. It is essential to frame why this debt bomb needs the fervent attention of every leader.

The G20's Debt Service Suspension Initiative (DSSI), as a case in point, provided limited relief for some countries post the

Covid pandemic. However, the overall G20 Common Framework for Debt Treatments hasn't yet shown effectiveness in solving debt crises quickly and efficiently.

Debt in Africa has always been intertwined with colonial exploitation via lenders from the 'Paris Club', the IMF, and the World Bank and a new debt scene that includes China, Saudi Arabia, and various private sources.

Leaders must remain acutely aware that there is no money that comes without cost and obligation. The repayment of this debt will be taken in generational enslavement of the continent's people and resources. Is the short-term relief of badly structured debt worth the ultimate price?

Transformative, sober, and focused thinking is critically needed to prevent the deepening of the debt crisis. Importantly, these problems must be approached from a sense of leading beyond now. African leaders across public and private spaces must act differently to move away from a permanent state of indebtedness and its accompanying chokehold on economies.

Sources: https://data.one.org/data-dives/debt/ ; IMF Debt Sustainability Analysis ; World Bank International Debt Statistics ;

Helpless Aid

Since decolonisation in the mid 20th century, many African nations have received substantial amounts of foreign 'aid' - either bilaterally from western nations, or through international institutions. Initially, this 'aid' was presented as a means to help newly independent countries establish themselves, address infrastructure deficits, and foster development; all seemingly benign, except that 'aid' manifests a variety of problems.

Dependency

A key critique is that continuous aid deliberately fosters dependency, wherein African nations rely on foreign assistance instead of building robust domestic economic and political systems.

Governance

With aid often comes conditions and influence. Critics argue that this dynamic can undermine local governance as leaders prioritise donor demands over citizens' needs.

Economic stagnation

Aid suppresses economic growth. Countries focus on receiving aid rather than cultivating industries or pursuing policies that foster economic advancement.

More trade, less aid

Driving intra African trade and global trade partnerships boost economic growth. Initiatives like the African Continental Free Trade Area (AfCFTA) have the potential to unify markets, stimulate growth and end dependency on aid and debt.

Invest in human capital

Focusing on education, skill development, and healthcare empower populations to participate more effectively in the global economy.

Infrastructure development

Investments in infrastructure like roads, ports, and technology, make countries self-reliant.

Good governance

Transparent governance that fosters the rule of law, reduces corruption, and builds trust make nations more attractive for business and reduce reliance on aid.

Diversified economies

Diversifying economies away from single commodities or industries shield countries from global market fluctuations and create a broader base for economic growth

Local solution

Prioritising indigenous solutions to local problems instead of imported ideas or policies lead to more sustainable outcomes.

By leveraging trade, investing in people, and ensuring good governance, African leaders can create a more sustainable and prosperous outcomes if they develop the political will to break the aid dependency.

Technology Impetus

Across the continent, nations are harnessing the power of technology to transcend traditional developmental paradigms. By embracing innovations like mobile telecommunication, pioneering e-banking platforms, and dominating the mobile-money arena, and the step change impact of artificial intelligence, the continent can be poised for a technological renaissance.

This transformation is spearheaded mainly by indigenous innovation and entrepreneurial dynamism. It heralds the dawn of a more expansive evolution, with the anticipation of intercontinental free trade poised to amplify Africa's economic output to a staggering US$29 trillion by 2050.

In this panorama of progress, technology is not merely an enabler, but a cornerstone. Yet, a sobering reality tempers this optimism: Africa represents a mere 0.2 per cent of the global start-up value.

The continent grapples with fragmented markets and tenuous ties among crucial tech stakeholders, impeding its technological ascendancy.

The vitality of a start-up ecosystem hinges on the empowerment of its entrepreneurs, the availability of expansive capital, and a culture of collective knowledge dissemination while any progress requires intricate collaboration between policymakers, established business, and entrepreneurs.

For Africa to actualise its vast latent potential, envisioning a unified pan-African start-up community is desirable and an imperative. Such a synergistic network will be the backbone; fortifying and fostering the essential interconnections that will elevate Africa's burgeoning tech start-up landscape.

A paramount challenge of our times is multidimensional poverty; a plight that extends beyond monetary deprivation and touches on the essence of well-being. Addressing multidimensional poverty is not just a response, but an obvious revolutionary stride toward a luminous future. Embracing this mission could well be Africa's *magnum opus*, its unparalleled legacy to the world.

PART TWO

The Five Commitments

Commitment One

24

Become a Worthy Custodian

Commitment is not the absence of options

The Worthy Custodian emerges as a paragon of unyielding integrity, championing the collective's aspirations while adeptly steering through the tumultuous waters of an ever-transforming world. Without this resolute commitment, leaders are all-too susceptible to the intoxicating allure of superficial gratifications - those that serve personal enrichment and ego aggrandisement.

The lure of quick successes often overshadows the importance of lasting impact, as immediate gains can outshine the steadier progress of long-term sustainability. Commonly tragic is the enticement of clinging on to power, which eclipses the quest for holistic societal betterment, while the shimmering facade of wealth overshadows the intrinsic worth of moral rectitude. Such myopic perspectives are the precipice on which numerous organisations, communities, and nations teeter.

In this era, where socio-political and economic dynamics continuously evolve, the idea of a 'Worthy Custodian' emerges as an essential leadership archetype.

A Worthy Custodian is a beacon of integrity, safeguarding the interests of the collective while navigating the challenges of a shifting world. Such a figure is a paragon of impeccable virtue - a sentinel defending the collective's welfare amidst the tumultuous waves of change. Such leaders are known by their unrelenting dedication to their cause and steadfastness by which they work to serve in whatever capacity they have chosen.

They rise within communities and create an impact that outlives them for generations to come.

Worthy Custodians must be steeped in self-abnegation and unflinching responsibility, ensuring that the welfare and aspirations of their constituents remain paramount in every plan and decision.

For the archetypal custodian, this unwavering commitment to the collective defines their very essence. Despite the availability of easier paths, Worthy Custodians choose the rockier, steeper ascent.

A Worthy Custodian: Kenya's Wangari Muta Maathai

An iconic figure whose life was dedicated to transformative achievements; Maathai's legacy will resonate for centuries to come. Her passion for the environment and democracy fuelled her actions. In her pursuit of justice, she vociferously voiced her concerns about African poverty, emphasising that a society marked by extreme inequality was unacceptable. In 1977, Maathai founded the Green Belt Movement, a visionary initiative aimed at reforesting Kenya, breaking the cycle of poverty, and promoting harmony. She recognised the interconnectedness of environmental degradation, poverty, and conflict, and her motto 'The more you degrade the environment, the more you dig deeper into poverty', resonated with millions.

Her influence was monumental. Rallying Kenyans, especially women, Maathai spearheaded the planting of over 30 million trees, inspiring a global movement. The United Nations took notice and launched a tree-planting campaign that has led to the planting of an astounding 11 billion trees worldwide. More than 900,000 Kenyan women directly benefited from her efforts, finding empowerment through the sale of tree seedlings for reforestation.

Beyond her green initiatives, Maathai understood the power of political leadership for social progress. She boldly used the tree as a symbol of democratic struggle, leading protests against oppressive regimes. Her activism even provoked the ire of then-president Daniel arap Moi, who resorted to derogatory labels in the face of her resilience. Despite facing violence and adversity, Maathai remained unyielding in her convictions.

She addressed the UN on several occasions and spoke on behalf of women at special sessions of the General Assembly for the five-year review of the Earth Summit. She served on the commission for Global Governance and Commission on the Future. She and the Green Belt Movement have received numerous awards, most notably The 2004 Nobel Peace Prize.

Wangari Muta Maathai's commitment is a testament to the incredible impact one individual can have on the world. Her vision, determination, and indomitable spirit continue to inspire generations, reminding us that through compassion, activism, and unity, we can create lasting change and a more equitable world for all.

Sources:
https://www.nobelprize.org/prizes/peace/2004/maathai/biographical/#; Global Org of African Women. http://goawworld.org/index.php/en/

Rather than succumbing to the seductive allure of narcissistic endeavours, temporary accolades, or the appeal of transient riches, a Worthy Custodian is epitomised by the lasting impact they create through selflessness, unwavering accountability, and a monomaniacal focus on the greater good. This holistic perspective, though ambitious, is neither nebulous nor unattainable.

Anchoring Principle One: Uproot Systemic Prejudice

The noble role of a guardian in leadership does not merely reside in high-level strategic decisions. It deeply intertwines with the ethical mandate to cast a protective shield around the most vulnerable groups in society, safeguarding those susceptible to societal pitfalls, while recognising vulnerability as an innate human experience.

Protection, in this context, goes beyond mere physical safety. It envelops a broader spectrum of rights, including unhindered access to fundamental human rights, holistic healthcare, potable water, nourishing sustenance, an empowering educational foundation, and a thriving economy. These facets, seemingly elementary, remain elusive to a significant proportion of African society, mainly due to entrenched systemic prejudices and irresponsible leadership.

Any leader who finds prejudice in a system they oversee and leaves the bias intact or, even further entrenched, is not only an unworthy custodian, but they are also a dangerous one. 'This is how it has always been' is the weakest, most feeble defence to not tackling injustice, corruption, crime, racism, xenophobia, and any number of injustices contrived by humanity to cause each other harm. A leader's calculated apathy or brazen neglect in addressing these alarming disparities go beyond mere oversight. It represents a grievous betrayal of the custodial mandate. When systemic biases persist under the nose of those entrusted to dismantle them, it is a blatant display of ineptitude and a perilous act of perpetuating harm.

The enlightened leader understands that challenging and, ultimately, eradicating these biases is more than a duty. It is a moral imperative.

Anchoring Principle Two: Embrace Accountability

The very essence of leadership hinges upon the sacred bond of trust. Think of the implicit trust bestowed upon a caretaker when leaving a child in the care of others. Imagine then the profound sense of betrayal if the caretaker not only evades responsibility when things go awry, but audaciously exploits the situation for unsavoury gains.

Though seemingly simplistic, this allegory encapsulates a deeply unsettling leadership dilemma of our times: the overwhelming propensity of those in power to circumvent accountability. Such behaviour doesn't just erode trust, it undermines the very foundations of transparent governance.

Leadership is rented. Authentic leadership is sustained through accountability. Consider it the 'rent' leaders owe people. When leaders lack transparency, shirk responsibility, or perpetuate acts that are dishonest, they default on this rent, meriting their eviction. Yet, we often witness leaders extending their stay, occupying roles without the rightful mandate or genuine endorsement.

The essence of the Worthy Custodian paradigm lies in the acknowledgment and acceptance that leadership, in its essence, is both sacred and transient. Without this understanding, the corridors of power become a breeding ground for abuse. Genuine, transformative leadership thrives when accountability becomes its lifeblood - a moral 'rent' that leaders owe constituents.

Anchoring Principle Three: Serve the Right People

The road to impactful leadership necessitates unwavering clarity with respect to the communities you choose to serve. Those who lose sight of this compass often resort to dubious tactics to sustain their positions. However, it is paramount to recognise that the primary duty isn't toward shareholders or political cronies, but to the end beneficiaries - the populace or the consumer.

The heart-wrenching episode of an international aerospace giant- Boeing, which sacrificed its core values on the altar of stock market gains, is a grim testament to the hazards of skewed priorities. The aftermath - planes plummeting and over 300 lives tragically lost -stands as a haunting reminder of the dire consequences of leadership myopia.

Understanding who you serve and being committed to doing so, changes your entire leadership ethos. From eloquent speeches on campaign trails to polished pitches during job interviews, leaders frequently exhibit a tendency towards overpromising. This is not necessarily rooted in a lack of belief in their ability to fulfil their promises.

Contrarily, it stems from an overly magnanimous assessment of their competencies. To assert that one can singularly stimulate job creation without a comprehensive grasp of the intricate variables at play, or to pledge simultaneous profit delivery and total stakeholder satisfaction, borders on misleading representation. Such overpromises risk undermining one's leadership credibility. What matters most is to embrace decisions authentically.

Decision Checkpoints

In pursuit of alignment with the ethos of a Worthy Custodian, leaders should normalise asking these questions in their decision-making process:

Integrity and protection of vulnerable populations
Am I making this decision in the best interest of the most vulnerable communities and am I addressing any systemic biases that may affect them?

Accountability and transparent governance
If the details of this decision were made public, could I defend its integrity and its alignment with the broader mission of my leadership?

Dismantling prejudices and prioritising marginalised groups
Does this decision actively challenge and aim to rectify existing prejudices or imbalances, or could it inadvertently perpetuate them?

Serving true stakeholders
Who primarily benefits from this decision? Is it the broader community, end consumers or the electorate, or does it disproportionately favour a select few?

Leading Beyond Now impact
What are the generational repercussions of this decision? Does it prioritise fleeting gains or contribute to lasting, sustainable impact?

The Worthy Custodian archetype isn't a quixotic aspiration. It is a tangible recalibration of leadership ethos, urgently mandated by our present-day context. Such a leader is both a visionary and a pragmatist, understanding that authentic leadership transcends fleeting triumphs.

This quality of custodianship is about crafting a legacy anchored in unwavering integrity, transparent accountability, and an undying commitment to service.

Commitment Two

Responsibility with Influence

Influence, when wielded without care

casts shadows;

when used responsibly

illuminates paths

Influence is a potent currency for leaders. Every leader has power - the ability to shape others' thoughts and beliefs in a way that influences their future actions, either directly or indirectly. Often, this influence is clearly visible through the leader's instructions or commands. By any delineation, influence therefore equates to power.

In the theatre of ambition, many individuals gravitate towards leadership with a desire for the authority to shape people, systems, and policies according to their personal design. Contemporary seekers of power often covet the mantle of leadership without embracing the profound transformation requisite to epitomise genuine leadership. This disjunction between the pretence and the actual embodiment of leadership has precipitated the widespread militarisation of influence on an international scale.

With the acquisition of power and influence comes an implicit moral contract: to act in ways that champion the collective good, all the while moving organisations, communities, or nations forward. True leadership means making choices based on what is best for everyone, not just what makes one look good. This requires the leader to embrace inclusivity, marrying it seamlessly with the often-arduous task of decision-making.

In the rapidly changing world, key elements define the essence of effective, purpose-driven leadership such as: deliberate use of power, genuine promotion of diversity and inclusion, and strong systems for managing influence.

These core principles are crucial cornerstones for leaders striving for enduring impact. Collectively, these principles advocate for a brand of leadership that is not just future-focused but is rooted deeply in the lessons of the past and the imperatives of the present. They emphasise leaders' profound responsibility: to wield influence judiciously, champion inclusivity genuinely, and establish self-regulating frameworks that uphold ethical integrity.

Responsible with Influence: DRC's Dikembe Mutombo

While he made a name for himself in the NBA as a towering presence known for his shot-blocking prowess and defensive skills, his legacy extends far beyond the realm of sports. Dikembe Mutombo is a well-known humanitarian with a profound commitment to improving the lives of people, particularly in his native Democratic Republic of Congo. In 1997, Mutombo took a momentous step by founding the Dikembe Mutombo Foundation.

This foundation became his vehicle for driving change in his homeland. Over the years, his tireless efforts and unwavering dedication have earned him numerous accolades and recognition. Dikembe Mutombo extended his reach beyond the borders of the United States. In 2004, he participated in the Basketball Without Borders NBA program, where he and other NBA stars toured Africa, using basketball as a tool to improve infrastructure and spread awareness about the sport.

Mutombo's compassion and generosity know no bounds. He personally funded uniforms and expenses for the then Zaire women's basketball team during the 1996 Centennial Olympic Games in Atlanta, demonstrating his commitment to empowering the youth of his homeland. Mutombo's impact extends even further through his role as a spokesman for the international relief agency CARE and as the first youth emissary for the United Nations Development Program. These roles have allowed him to advocate for vital humanitarian causes on a global stage.

One of his enduring passions is supporting the Special Olympics. Mutombo became a Global Ambassador and a member of the Special Olympics International Board of Directors, championing the cause of Unified Sports, which brings people with and without intellectual disabilities together.

He has been recognised for his tireless efforts to reduce polio globally and improve the health of underserved populations in the Democratic Republic of Congo

In an age where leadership is often tested by its adaptability and vision, responsibility with influence is a vital beacon, illuminating the path for those, like Mutombo, who dare to lead beyond the comforts or constraints of the present into the vast potentialities of the future.

Anchoring Principle One: Be Positively Intentional with Power

By its very nature, leadership is multifaceted, delineating roles between leaders and those they serve. While such dexterity can function effectively, issues arise when individuals in leadership roles exert oppressive authority over those they guide. Such a 'power-over' leadership style can become embedded within an institution, and, like a spark, can quickly ignite a blaze. This propensity to exert control over others provides a dopamine surge in many humans - making it a tempting leadership style despite the existence of more evolved approaches.

The consortium Just Associates (JASS), a fusion of activists, educators, and scholars, offers an insightful categorisation of power into two primary domains: dominating power and positive and transformative power.

Dominating Power

Those in control of resources and decision making can exert influence over the less privileged and can marginalise them from resources, autonomy, safety, and active participation shown through three power windows.

Visible power

This involves state apparatuses and formalised political structures exercised through laws, policies, and institutional decision making.

Hidden power

This refers to organised interests, both legitimate and covert, that covertly manipulate decisions, resources, media and security to serve and safeguard their interests.

Invisible power

This aspect encompasses the deep-seated beliefs, cultural norms, and societal values that mould an individual's perception of 'normality' or 'rightness.' It also includes strategically exploiting these beliefs to validate specific political ideologies and actions, even when violent.

Regrettably, the allure of unchecked power remains pervasive worldwide, not solely within Africa. This dominance is a testament to why, despite the sheer irrationality and zero-sum essence of war, the self-styled paragons of civilisation still engage in armed confrontations. Whether directly or through covert means, they supply weapons and sponsor extremism, fostering chaos. This veil allows Western and Eastern actors to exploit Africa's resources with impunity, showing little regard for the economic, environmental, social, or cultural ramifications on the affected nations.

Positive and Transformative Power

In contrast to dominating power, positive power does not solely manifest as a tool for domination or suppression; it can be a conduit for collective action, fostering liberation and metamorphosis. Instead of emulating dominating power paradigms, we can foster a power dynamic grounded in equality, inclusivity, and emancipation.

JASS labels this as transformative power:

Power within

This refers to the intrinsic capability to dream, believe, innovate, and problem-solve. It is the force that compels individuals to voice concerns and take action.

Power with

This focuses on collaboration, building solidarity rooted in mutual respect, understanding differences, and pursuing shared goals.

Power to

This aspect embodies the potential to enact change, transform lives, and incrementally challenge established norms.

Power for

This captures our collective aspirations, guiding principles, and the vision for the future we strive to realise.

Africa stands on the precipice of embracing transformative power. Straddling the realms of retracing historical steps and carving a pioneering path forward, Africa's journey is not - and should not - be linear. The disparities in developmental trajectories across nations on the continent demand generational commitment and unified leadership to bridge the gaps.

What is both commonplace and predictably disheartening is observing leaders who employ 'power over' to scale their chosen ladder, only to ultimately be 'dethroned' - often at the behest of even more powerful adversaries. Such leaders, metaphorically, live and 'perish' by the same sword.

A legacy built in the wrong direction

Robert Mugabe's tumultuous leadership was not a sudden devolution towards its end; it was the very foundation of his ascent. His calculated acts, such as the post-independence massacre of thousands of people during the Gukurahundi genocide, weren't solely displays of tribal supremacy, but were messages asserting his unyielding dominance.

Yet, after nearly four decades marred by economic, social, and political turmoil, his downfall came from insiders - protégés moulded in his likeness. The impact of this, and many other acts of Mugabe's orchestration, have and will continue to bestride generations - shaped by loss, marginalisation, and the inevitable mass migration.

Leaders nurtured in an environment that laud 'power over' not only perpetuate, but intensify this autocratic style, crafting their unique signature of tyranny. The realm of 'power over' is the preserve of tyrants across political, social, and corporate landscapes - an ending invariably presaged by history.

Anchoring Principle Two: Cultivate Diversity and Inclusion with Authenticity

Embracing responsibility when wielding influence epitomises the harmonious blend of power with, to, and for. This synergy can only be actualised when those at the helm possess a profound sense of inner strength and empowerment - often referred to as 'power within'.

Our global narrative, and within the African continent, reveals deep-seated tribal, economic, religious, and cultural prejudices. These divisive sentiments are not inherent but are often incited and exacerbated by leaders who strategically exploit them. For decades, leadership within and outside the continent has perpetuated myths of tribal, racial, or economic exceptionalism, driving wedges between communities.

Entire 'civilisations' have developed wealth on - literally - the blood, sweat, and tears of exploitation: slavery, colonisation, extermination, and genocide. Almost all corridors of power globally echo the sentiment and build their policies around divisiveness, separation, and oppression.

However, a reflection upon nature reveals the undeniable potency of inclusivity and diversity. Just as an ecosystem thrives with varied species, human societies flourish when enriched with a plethora of perspectives and experiences.

The absence of such diversity culminates in an echo chamber reminiscent of genetic inbreeding. Such homogenisation weakens our species' genetic vigour and impoverishes human discourse, leading to stagnation in critical thought, a dearth of empathy, and a myopic worldview.

Those who genuinely seek to chart a future-oriented course, intentionally champion diversity and inclusivity across their establishments. They recognise that the richness of diverse thought and experience engenders innovation, resilience, and adaptability.

To harness power effectively, it must be channelled toward the collective good, not wielded as a weapon of subjugation. Leaders ought to acknowledge and respect the latent influence inherent within those they lead. For in the realm of leadership, a fundamental truth prevails: those who are served wield the ultimate power - the choice to cease being guided. A populace that progressively awakens to its intrinsic power and recognises its available options can pivot, redefining where and to whom they pledge their allegiance.

Additionally, leaders must resist the temptation to externalise their animosities. Resorting to mercenaries - be it literal hitmen or institutional proxies that suppress dissent - indicates a leadership style that prioritises silencing over engaging. Such strategies, rooted in confrontation rather than dialogue, signal leadership on the brink.

When leaders consistently view elimination as the sole recourse to counteract dissent, their tenure becomes precariously ephemeral.

Anchoring Principle Three: Robust Systems for Influence Regulation

At the heart of every flourishing civilisation is the bedrock of systemic order - a lattice of carefully curated mechanisms that harmoniously channel the energies of its constituents. A well-architected system has the power to cultivate a virtuous cycle, nurturing ethical aspirants of power.

Conversely, a poorly designed structure can inadvertently evolve into an adept conveyor, churning out a ceaseless torrent of myopic, self-serving opportunists -whether for hire or, as circumstances might dictate, for electoral mandates. Embracing the tenets of 'Leading Beyond Now' necessitates the conscientious creation of self-regulatory frameworks.

These systems should not merely be designed to function effectively, but must be imbued with the capacity to promote virtuous behaviour and swiftly identify and rectify malevolent tendencies. While challenging in design, such proactive systems are within the realms of human ingenuity.

History offers ample testimony to this: civilisations, in their evolutionary trajectory, have instinctively woven into their sociocultural tapestry mechanisms that restrain, if not deter, those with divisive predispositions from gaining ascendancy.

It is evident that more than the mere presence of a system is required. Its efficiency and efficacy lie in the nimbleness with which it operates. African and global institutions that stand as paragons of governance are characterised by their adeptness in eliminating any components that betray their foundational principles. Whether it be leaders, employees, contractors, or suppliers - any entity that fails to align with the institutional ethos or engages in exploitative behaviour is swiftly realigned or, if necessary, ejected.

Yet, a disconcerting anomaly seems to plague the political and public spheres, particularly in Africa. Instead of mirroring the self-correcting dynamics observed in well-governed institutions, these arenas have, somewhat perplexingly, mastered the craft of not only retaining individuals of questionable competence and integrity, but also magnetically drawing such personalities into their fold.

It begs the question: *Why?* The answer may lie partly in the deeply entrenched legacies of post-colonial administrative systems, which may not have been adequately recalibrated to cater to the unique socio-cultural and vast political dynamics of the continent. Alternatively, it could be symptomatic of a more pervasive global trend where populist sentiments sometimes overshadow reasoned deliberations, leading to the elevation of personalities over principles. Whatever the root cause, the onus rests upon the current generation of thinkers, leaders, and change-makers to introspect and innovate.

Crafting a durable and adaptive system requires incorporating both timeless wisdom and avant-garde insights. Traditional knowledge systems can offer profound understanding of communal harmony and conflict resolution, while contemporary technological advancements, such as artificial intelligence and blockchain, might provide tools for ensuring transparency, accountability, and participatory governance.

In essence, creating a robust system isn't a mere administrative task - it is an intentional and continuous journey of refinement. Only by marrying the lessons of the past with the present innovations can societies hope to craft frameworks that, while facilitating the aspirations of the virtuous, leave no room for the ascent of the unscrupulous.

Decision Checkpoints

In the pursuit of this commitment, leaders should normalise asking these questions:

Intentionality with power

Am I exercising my influence to empower and uplift those I lead, or am I merely using it to consolidate my position and power?

Authenticity in inclusivity

In making this decision, have I genuinely considered diverse perspectives and ensured inclusivity, or am I unconsciously perpetuating singular narratives and biases?

Robust systems for influence regulation

Does this decision bolster a self-regulatory and transparent system that encourages ethical behaviour while swiftly addressing malpractices?

Service over suppression

Am I choosing engagement and collaboration over confrontation, and service over suppression, in my approach to this challenge or opportunity?

Leading Beyond Now impact

How does this decision reflect my commitment to 'leading beyond now', and what legacy will it create for future generations and the overarching ethos of my country, organisation, or community?

Commitment Three

Curate Wise Counsel

Wisdom is not merely gained through our own journey but is enriched by the insights and experiences of those walking beside us

For leaders to navigate the labyrinth of decision-making, it is paramount to procure sagacious advice. This allows them to harness a myriad of perspectives, all rich in knowledge and depth. A prevailing quandary many leaders grapple with is the inadvertent gravitation towards confidants who solely resonate with their viewpoints, thereby fostering an insular echo chamber that stifles innovation and breadth of thought.

To transcend this impediment, leaders ought to be meticulous in creating a circle of diverse individuals with the capability to proffer invaluable insights and question established notions. Additionally, they must be receptive to assimilating knowledge from a vast spectrum of sources, including from those who may not occupy influential roles.

Curating wise counsel is neither a surrogate nor an elixir for inherent wisdom.

The primary role of such counsel is to serve as a touchstone for ideas, a crucible for critical evaluation, and a bulwark against the pitfalls of homogenous thinking. History offers ample testament to leaders who commenced their journey with judicious counsel but, over time, replaced those luminaries with pliant 'advisors,' thus succumbing to the whims of their inadequacies.

Soliciting sagacious guidance is a linchpin for leaders to include multifaceted viewpoints and enlightened recommendations in their decision-making process. Nonetheless, an inherent pitfall that traps these leaders is the seduction of surrounding themselves exclusively with sycophantic voices, thus unwittingly creating an echo chamber, reverberating solely their own sentiments, and constricting the spectrum of insights.

The poignancy of seeking counsel lies in its capacity to act as a sounding board, to incisively critique, and to forestall the perils of homogenised thinking. Such thinking merely serves as ceremonial endorsement, unreflectively validating the caprices of the leadership, irrespective of its competence or lack thereof.

A Curator of Wise Counsel: Sudan's Mo Ibrahim

Mo Ibrahim, renowned for his transformative contributions in the telecommunications sector and his laudable initiatives in African governance, exemplifies the epitome of a leader who ardently values and meticulously implements the principles of curating wise counsel. His endeavours manifest a profound commitment to elevating governance and leadership standards, demonstrating the invaluable significance of cultivating a multifaceted repository of wisdom and insights.

Ibrahim has consistently assembled platforms where the counsel of a diverse spectrum of seasoned and sagacious individuals leveraging and share their unique experiences and insights. His belief in the power of failure as a profound teacher aligns seamlessly with the idea that one enlightened by diverse experiences offers invaluable perspectives.

Under Ibrahim's aegis, the Mo Ibrahim Foundation has championed inclusive and broad-based stakeholder engagement, ensuring a plethora of voices are heard, respected, and considered in the dialogues surrounding African governance.

In the context of curating wise counsel, phronesis plays a crucial role in guiding individuals to make sound decisions by discerning the practical and ethical dimensions of the advice they receive, ultimately helping them choose the most prudent course of action.

Anchoring Principle One: Assemble a Coterie of the Sagacious

Gleaning insights from judicious, unbiased sages is an investment that often proves less costly than the repercussions of uninformed decisions. Leaders benefit profoundly from a sanctuary wherein ideas are tested and candid, even unsolicited, feedback on their initiatives and strategies is welcomed.

This conclave of the erudite should encompass individuals who have traversed the spectrum of success and adversity and emerged resilient.

The insights of one who has risen from the ashes of failure are often richer than those borne from a series of uncontested triumphs. Such figures serve as anchors, offering perspective and grounding. As the adage goes, only a fool would gauge a river's depth using both their feet.

Anchoring Principle Two: Establish an Aural Observatory

Dedicate a space for the voices of your community. The draw of such an observatory lies in its capacity to harness insights from myriad sources and echelons. Recognising that wisdom is not tethered to age, position, or wealth is pivotal. By virtue of diligent listening, a leader is invariably positioned for judicious decision-making. While not always culminating in tangible action, the act of listening serves as a reliable barometer, reflecting the efficacy or potential shortcomings of one's leadership.

However, the landscape of seeking and imparting counsel is riddled with challenges. The seeker and the provider of advice must transcend innate biases, such as an overweening penchant for their own viewpoints, irrespective of their validity. Additionally, genuine listening is an intricate ballet of patience and discernment, requiring a generous investment of time and effort.

Anchoring Principle Three: Be Deliberate in Your Associations

The conscious curating of one's inner circle is a potent mechanism for self-regulation. A pervasive peril in leadership is that insecurity often begets a tendency for surrounding oneself with admirers rather than those unencumbered by allegiance.

Tragically, as one ascends in stature, the calibre of associates often dwindles, amplifying the spectre of homogenous thinking. Leaders should mitigate this by intentionally fostering connections spanning from the grassroots to the elite, ensuring that voices from the most marginalised to the most empowered are included in your sphere of influence.

Decision Checkpoints

In pursuit of alignment with the ethos of Curating Wise Counsel, leaders should normalise asking these questions in their decision-making process:

Assessing wisdom sources

Have I consulted a diverse array of individuals, especially those who have weathered both success and adversity, to gain multifaceted insights on this matter?

Bias and subjectivity

Am I favouring advice that merely resonates with my pre-existing beliefs, or am I truly considering counsel based on its merit, even if it challenges my initial stance?

Evaluating feedback mechanisms

Do the feedback mechanisms I've established reflect both the acclaim and critique of my leadership, ensuring I'm not in an echo chamber of constant affirmation?

Circle of influence

Have I carefully considered the individuals I surround myself with? Are they enhancing and challenging my perspective, or merely reinforcing my existing viewpoints and decisions?

Leading Beyond Now impact

Have I put in place systems that will push my successor to curate wise counsel?

Commitment Four

Be Curious

**The loathing of discomfort
spurs the curious
to innovate**

The octopus, a creature of aquatic wonder, navigates the depths with heart - three hearts, to be precise. Three hearts that orchestrate the symphony of its existence. This anatomical trio is far from mere redundancy; it is a testament to the intricate dance of survival woven into the very fabric of nature. In this aqueous realm, redundancy is not a frivolous extravagance - it's a lifeline.

As an octopus embarks on its ventures, these three hearts are more than mere pumps. They're a strategic ensemble designed to navigate the challenges of an ever-changing aquatic world.

The first heart beats with intensity, circulating life-giving blood through the gills, where oxygen is harvested from the water. With each rhythmic surge, oxygen courses through the octopus, nourishing its body and fuelling its pursuits.

The second heart, near the gills, drives the oxygen-enriched blood to the rest of the creature's anatomy. This pulse sustains the octopus, empowering it to manoeuvre gracefully and precisely through the water's expanse.

And then there's the third heart, a sentinel of purpose, responsible for circulating blue, copper-based blood throughout the octopus's system. This rich hue is a testament to the presence of hemocyanin - a molecule that cradles oxygen with an embrace not unlike our own iron-bearing haemoglobin.

But why this threefold arrangement? Redundancy, it turns out, is the artisan of adaptation. Surprises lurk around every coral-clad corner in the ocean's watery labyrinth. An octopus's world is a canvas of shifting currents, hidden predators, and fleeting opportunities. And so, these three hearts - each attuned to a different rhythm - ensure that, even if one falters, the harmonious cadence of survival endures.

In this, we glimpse a profound truth: nature weaves its tales with an orchestra of backup plans. Redundancy isn't a whimsical flourish, it's a masterstroke of resilience. Just as a mariner's vessel is fortified against the fury of storms, an octopus's being is fortified against the capricious currents of its environment.

So, as we marvel at the three hearts that beat within an octopus, let us recognise the wisdom of nature's design. It is a design that teaches us the invaluable lesson of preparedness - a lesson that echoes through the waves and across the landscapes of existence.

Without inbuilt redundancy, failure can be devastating.

Life in Africa is far more complex than many acknowledge. To truly comprehend this complexity, we must resist oversimplifying our perceptions. Embracing the continent's inherent antifragility allows for solutions that strengthen collective resilience rather than denying its multifaceted nature. A society or nation's antifragility is a testament to its adaptability and growth potential, not stagnation.

Nassim Nicholas Taleb conceptualised 'antifragility' as that which benefits from disorder. Rather than merely resisting adversities, antifragility thrives on them. The core of Taleb's argument is that we should structure our societies, lives, and institutions in ways that *benefit* from disorder instead of merely trying to predict or prevent it. The world is inherently unpredictable, and antifragility provides a way to navigate and thrive amidst this unpredictability.

A Life of Curiosity and Antifragility

Zimbabwe's Chido Govera

Chido Govera's remarkable life exemplifies the concept of antifragility, where adversity becomes the catalyst for not just survival but for an inspiring transformation that empowers others. Born in Zimbabwe in 1986, Chido's early years were marked by daunting challenges. At the age seven, she tragically lost her mother to AIDS, leaving her and her younger brother orphaned under her grandmother's care. Yet, the hardships didn't stop there. Chido endured family abuse and economic hardship, compelling her to leave school at the age of nine. Her days were dedicated to gruelling work in the fields, all in pursuit of a meagre portion of maize meal.

But at the age of ten, an opportunity emerged that would forever alter the course of Chido's life. She had the chance to attend a transformative week-long program at Africa University in Mutare, Zimbabwe. This program endowed her with a remarkable skill: cultivating oyster mushrooms using corn stalk waste products.

This newfound knowledge wasn't just about food; it was a pathway to a better life, not only for herself but for the countless others who would follow in her footsteps. With unwavering determination, Chido embraced her newfound skill and turned it into a mission.

Chido didn't want to be the sole beneficiary of her knowledge; she aspired to be a guiding light for others, particularly for orphans, women, and girls facing circumstances similar to her own early struggles. In 2013, she took a monumental step and founded the Future of Hope Foundation, dedicated to providing sustainable food, nutrition, and income security to those in need.

Mushroom farming became the linchpin of this mission, but Chido's vision extended far beyond that. The foundation's efforts broadened to encompass various areas, including the establishment of solarized water facilities, nutrition gardens, soil enhancement projects, as well as poultry and cattle farming. These initiatives were meticulously designed to help individuals break free from the clutches of poverty, offering them the chance to construct a more secure future.

Chido Govera's life story is a living testament to the power of resilience, determination, and a spirit of giving. She's transformed personal adversity into an enduring source of inspiration for those who have confronted hardship. Her journey vividly illustrates how one person's unwavering commitment to positive change can illuminate the path to a brighter, more secure future for individuals and communities in need.

Not just a survivor; she's a torchbearer of hope and a living example of the boundless impact of human compassion, embodying the antifragility of the human spirit, which not only withstands adversity but thrives and inspires others to do the same.

In charting a transformative path, three core principles emerge: The value of being antifragile, the role of exploration coupled with innovation, and the urgency to shun traditional dependencies.

Anchoring Principle One: Be Antifragile

In truth, certainty is an elusive state. We often rely on hopes, educated guesses, and calculated risks. Avoiding or addressing crises requires an inherent curiosity - about the origins, the affected people, and potential prevention and solutions. One must also be keenly interested in understanding its long-term impact and demonstrate readiness to take decisive action.

The enigma of the Zimbabwean economy exists within the realm of antifragility - where its very existence defies conventional comprehension. Even the most eminent economists are still trying to understand why and how this nation, perennially teetering on the precipice, has so far resisted complete collapse. The ceaseless onslaught of societal and economic oppression and upheavals has left an indelible imprint, a duality of fragility and fortitude. It is a juxtaposition both perplexing and poignant, as the constant shocks have, paradoxically, made threadbare the fabric of the nation while simultaneously endowing it with resilience. In the clash of chaos and chance, the Zimbabwean people endure, albeit within the constraints of a livelihood marred by inequities and inherent flaws - an existence where the ticking of survival echoes, unevenly.

The very reason Zimbabwe remains impervious to remedies is

the same reason it eludes - for now - a state of utter collapse. So far, however, this randomness has mostly benefited the unscrupulous. In the grand narrative of this nation, as in the more remarkable story of humanity, it is often the tumultuous forces of unpredictability that foster evolution. Zimbabwe will benefit from the emergence of committed, brave and curious leaders poised to metamorphose this uncertainty into an instrument of progress - a symposium where opportunity and equity come together. Only then will the Zimbabwean economic riddle reveal its ultimate significance - a testament not only to resilience but to the indomitable spirit that shapes the destiny of a people.

Across sectors, players in the economies of African states can embody several of Taleb's antifragile ethos.

Embrace volatility and chaos
Regular exposure to minor stressors can make systems (and people) stronger. Just like muscles grow stronger with stress and rest, systems can benefit from randomness and variability.

Reduce vulnerabilities
Instead of trying to predict exact future events (which is complex and often incorrect), focus on reducing vulnerabilities. This way, when unexpected events happen, systems are not overly exposed.

Overcompensation

Systems that overcompensate in response to stressors become stronger. The human body, for instance, overcompensates for moderate physical stress by building stronger muscles.

Decentralise

Large, centralised systems can be more vulnerable to systemic collapses while decentralised systems are more resilient and antifragile because problems can be isolated.

Redundancy is good

While redundancy might seem inefficient - like having two lungs – it is a form of insurance against the unexpected. Systems with redundancy are more robust and can be more antifragile.

Anchoring Principle Two: Exploration and Innovation - Twin Pillars of Growth

Curiosity is the progenitor of exploration and innovation. It's an attitude, a deliberate orientation towards the world, that births transformative practices. In positions of leadership and influence, managing resources necessitates a responsibility to channel them not just into exploration but also towards fostering innovation.

The essence of innovation lies in its ability to disrupt the status quo, look beyond the known, and craft solutions tailored to unique challenges. Those at the helm must prioritise and fund research, but also, and crucially, create environments that stimulate innovative thought, leading to tangible solutions.

The journey from intent to implementation can be bridged through committed focus on innovation, ensuring that Africa does not remain a mere consumer - and labour provider - of global advancements but emerges as a formidable innovator.

Bridging hope to Africa's youth in extremism's shadow
To unravel the generationally defining reality of Africa's youth - a demographic widely excluded from education, vocation, and employment - it is vital to embrace a fundamental truth: the future belongs to them, while we are but transient custodians.

If leaders accept this truth, then they are compelled to proactively engage with and enable the aspirations and challenges of the youth. Instead of arrogantly prescribing misguided solutions, our focus should shift towards nurturing an environment where the youth can flourish and thrive.

The current reality paints a starkly contrasting picture. The youth of Africa find themselves thrust into a dire circumstance marked by a sense of hopelessness, the stifling absence of a voice, dehumanising poverty, and leadership that chooses stone deafness to their pleas and bat blindness to their necessities.

Only those who've never faced the bleakness of destitution can view extremism and radicalisation through the skewed lens of judgement and assumption.

Recognising that options are limited for those mired in utter deprivation is crucial. Judgement is a luxury the privileged can ill-afford, yet they are recklessly extravagant with it.

From a pragmatic and moral standpoint, investing in the fundamental infrastructure needed for economic growth proves far more cost-effective than channelling resources into military equipment for security measures and counteracting extremism. The ominous spectre of sponsored terrorism persists because, regrettably, conflict is often the preferred smokescreen for covert operations.

The path forward demands a radical shift. Solutions should not be unilaterally imposed upon the youth but should be collaboratively conceived alongside them. More profoundly, empowerment should be the cornerstone. Just as a series of negligent tenants can render a structure dilapidated and frail, mismanagement can similarly erode the very promise that our youth hold.

Recalibration is in order - one where the youth's aspirations are recognised and celebrated, their potential isn't squandered but harnessed, and their voices aren't silenced but amplified. The future is theirs. Our role as Worthy Custodians is to nurture their growth, building a foundation that transcends ephemeral concerns and paves the way for lasting progress.

Fuelling a revolution

There's an entrepreneurial revolution starting to happen in Africa's economically challenged nations, but there's a catch. A handful of vital ingredients must come together to ignite this economic firework. And while every region has its own unique factors, some universal strategies can make this entrepreneurial revolution take off.

Imagine having the next big idea but not a dime to kickstart it. The barriers of access to financial resources need to be intentionally removed for the upliftment of youth entrepreneurs. Reliable internet, healthcare, roads, electricity - not luxury, but the basic foundation for economic upliftment.

Knowledge applied is power. To equip the daring, what the youth need are ecosystems of knowledge, infrastructure, access to digital tools and enabling support – not AK47s.

Anchoring Principle Three: Independence from Traditional Dependencies

History stands testament to the power structures dictating global narratives. Rule-making and rule-breaking often serve the interests of a privileged few. However, for tangible progression, risks are indispensable.

African countries' proper progression will unlock when they begin to assert their independence from the traditional international development actors - who are fundamental instruments of covert power distribution and sub-diplomatic interventions to pressure political outcomes beneficial to their handlers.

African states need to eliminate dependencies on these external entities. The true essence of leadership here will be formulating policies prioritising self-sustainability, harnessing domestic resources, and focusing on homegrown solutions. Such a pathway ensures that African countries are not bound by external agendas, but are free to charter unique courses

While the international community remains an ally, Africa must pivot from being a beneficiary to an equal partner, cultivating collaborations that serve mutual interests and severing those that do not.

Those steering the change must resonate deeply with the grassroots challenges. This ensures that solutions are not mere top-down impositions but are crafted in tandem with ground realities.

For genuine emancipation, certain established norms need re-evaluation. A leadership that hesitates to break societal and economic chains can never truly liberate.

A nation's trove of mineral wealth often casts a paradoxical shadow on its societal fabric, intertwining it with radicalism, internal strife, economic disparities, and periods of stagnation. This complex web reveals a dual nature - fragility juxtaposed with antifragility. For a transformative trajectory, a meticulous reassessment and reconstruction of the prevailing rules of engagement are imperative.

Certain norms, rather than fostering growth, stagnate and suppress the collective. These include oppressive rules crafted to favour a select few, hierarchical structures that limit upward mobility and constraints that deny individuals the right to exercise control over their possessions.

A tenure in leadership that does not challenge and dismantle such restraints is not just a missed opportunity but a tacit endorsement of suppression. Failure to do this is, arguably, either inept or malevolent - and tragically, frequently both.

This continent can craft a narrative of unparalleled growth by embracing antifragility, championing exploration and innovation, and seeking independence from traditional development actors.

To realise a vision, society must exhibit collective temperance against not just greed, but all vices that shackle its progress. It is fundamental to bolster the moral compass, to stand upright with integrity and steadfast purpose. An invaluable lesson for Africa's vast populace is the inherent power within everyone. Whether it be self-determination, innate value, or the potency of one's voice, every individual wields leverage that can be used for negotiation and change.

The individuals most adept at discerning the multifaceted challenges faced by the youth or the elderly are, invariably, the youth and the elderly themselves. They must be entrenched on both ends of the decision-making spectrum.

Africa's elite are drawn to events like Davos, which, amidst other elite conclaves, have been criticised for their seemingly detached discussions. Despite their prestigious facades, these gatherings often appear to be echo chambers for the affluent, theorising solutions for challenges they have yet to personally experience. Hobnobbing and often oblivious uncaring or both, to the transformative impact these funds could have on education, healthcare, or technological advancement. The positive impact on the economies they gather to dissect and judge is virtually untraceable.

Decision Checkpoints

In pursuit of actualising curiosity, leaders should normalise applying these check points to their decision making.

Embrace antifragility

How does this decision ensure that our institution or nation not only withstands challenges but evolves and strengthens from them?

Commitment to exploration and innovation

Have we allocated sufficient resources (both human and material) towards research, exploration, and innovative solutions, ensuring our decisions are informed and forward-thinking?

Independence from external development actors

Does this choice lead us towards self-sufficiency and reduce dependency on aid and global entities?

Leadership reflecting those served

To what extent does this decision resonate with the lived experiences and aspirations of the people we represent? Have we consulted and involved them adequately?

Leading Beyond Now impact

Does this decision defy any established norms and structures that historically have held back progress, ensuring a move toward equity?

Commitment Five

82

Tether Yourself to Noble Values

Without values nothing is sacred

Often that which propels us or holds us back is within our mind. The kind of people we are to those around us - and the kind of people we are as leaders all come from within. Like ink to water, your belief system colours every decision, every reaction, every choice and outcome.

Committing to oneself is a paradox. While it might seem to be an act of self-indulgence, in truth, it is the ultimate act of selflessness. To consciously chart the course of our identity means deconstructing the societal norms we've inherited and subsequently reconstructing a self-concept rooted in intentionality and, for the good of mankind, anchored to a worthy cause.

A Tethered Life - Namibia's Dr. Helena Ndume

Helena Ndume's life is a living testament to the embodiment of noble values. For over two decades, she has dedicated her life to a singular mission: to end preventable blindness and to illuminate a path to a brighter future for those who have lost their sight. Her unwavering commitment to this cause has touched the lives of over 30,000 individuals, with the majority of them being her fellow Namibians.

Growing up in South Africa during the apartheid era, Dr. Ndume bore witness to the injustices and inhumane living conditions that surrounded her. Determined to make the world a better place, she resolved to become a doctor, a decision that was rooted in her deep-seated desire to help others. She pursued her medical education in Germany and completed her fellowship in India, an experience that exposed her to the dire circumstances faced by thousands living in poverty due to preventable blindness.

Realising the global need for humanitarian eye care, Dr. Ndume returned to Namibia with a resolute commitment to restoring sight and providing a brighter future for those in need.

Under the banner of SEE International, Dr. Ndume has organized a minimum of five eye camps annually, reaching an estimated 1,000 individuals ranging from the young to the elderly. Her work has not been limited to her home country; she has undertaken sight-restoring missions in various nations, exemplifying her dedication to a global humanitarian cause.

Throughout her years of service, Dr. Ndume has received a series of prestigious awards, reflecting her remarkable contributions to humanity. She became the first recipient of the United Nations Nelson Rolihlahla Mandela Prize in 2015, a testament to her unwavering service to the betterment of humanity.

What sets Dr. Helena Ndume apart is not just her exceptional medical expertise but her indomitable spirit and the noble values that drive her. Her dedication to serving the less fortunate has restored hope and independence to thousands. Among the countless individuals whose sight she has restored, there are grandparents who can now gaze upon their grandchildren, mothers who can see their children's faces, individuals who can return to work and provide for their families, and children who can attend school.

Leadership isn't a birth right, nor are people born as leaders. It is a conscious evolution. A leader emerges from the crucible of self-reflection, shaped by the dual forces of self-acceptance and deliberate choices.

Anchoring Principle One: Revere Humanity

In an epoch where genuine human connections seem fleeting and the spirit of mutual respect wanes, there's an imperative to champion the essence of humanity. Long past is the time when the intrinsic values of dignity, respect, and the tenets of 'ubuntu' were ubiquitous. This guiding philosophy, symbolising our interconnectedness as 'I am because you/we are', is more relevant now than ever. The moral compass that separates the corruptible from the incorruptible is deeply rooted in value systems. While the corruptible gravitate toward transient gains, the incorruptible anchor themselves to fairness, justice, and intrinsic worth principles.

For leaders, the voyage without a compass - values, and

boundaries - is fraught with peril. Such individuals risk being tossed about by the tempests of circumstance, endangering not just themselves but all in their charge. Choosing the values to live by is to set an internal compass and a fortress, guiding one's journey and demarcating one's boundaries.

Anchoring Principle Two: Be Alive to your Ripple Effect

The annals of leadership are riddled with tales of triumph and tragedy, and one of the distinguishing traits between the two outcomes is empathy. It is alarming to note the tarnished perception of empathy in recent leadership paradigms, where it is erroneously equated with weakness. Empathy is not mere sentimentality; it is a bridge to understanding, a lens to perceive the multitudes of human experiences. This understanding paves the way for ethical decision-making, cultivates relationships, and sows the seeds of mutual respect. Leadership devoid of empathy is a hollow shell, often leading to decisions that prioritise the self over the collective, with dire consequences.

Leaders who can only get their point across through violence are irreparably unevolved and therefore misfits of society.

The vacuum left by the absence of empathy is dangerous, leading to societal ruptures, discrimination, and a host of ills. Ills that originate from the tragically long entrenched practice of dehumanisation - a deliberate erasure of one's humanity. Dehumanisation is far from benign; it is the progenitor of some of history's gravest injustices which, pathetically, still exist today.

Anchoring Principle Three: Incorruptibility

To understand incorruptibility, we must first acknowledge corruption in all its facets. Beyond the mere exchange of money for favours, corruption encompasses the erosion of moral integrity, the compromise of principles for personal gain, and the sacrifice of collective well-being for individual or sectional advantage. Incorruptibility, in contrast, is not merely the absence of corruption but an active commitment to upholding values and principles, even in the face of personal cost or societal pressure.

A leader's ethical foundation is the bedrock of their incorruptibility. This foundation comprises a matrix of principles, values, and beliefs that collectively determine the leader's moral compass. Every decision, every action, and every reaction is filtered through this matrix. A leader with a solid ethical foundation perceives their role as stewardship, a responsibility to serve others and the greater good rather than self-interest.

The path to leadership often traverses terrains fraught with temptations. These can range from material gains to power accumulation, from ego gratification to the seduction of unchecked authority. The pinnacle of incorruptibility is achieved when a leader consistently resists these temptations, recognising that succumbing to them diminishes their integrity and the trust placed in them by those they serve.

Incorruptibility is not only about individual integrity but also about creating an environment that actively discourages corruption. Incorruptible leaders prioritise transparency, promote checks and balances and foster a culture of openness and accountability. By embedding these principles into their operating DNA, leaders ensure that ethical conduct becomes the default rather than the exception.

Ignorance can sometimes be a precursor to corruptible behaviour. Leaders who seek to elevate themselves and their organisations to the heights of incorruptibility recognise the importance of continuous education and enlightenment. By fostering an environment of learning and self-improvement, they ensure that decisions are made based on knowledge, understanding and a profound respect for ethical boundaries.

Authentic leadership is as much about the present as the future; an acute awareness of the legacy to be left behind. Actions, decisions, and behaviours are informed by a vision of a future where ethical conduct is the norm, where organisations and societies thrive on trust and mutual respect, and corruption in all its forms is relegated to the annals of history.

Incorruptibility is the zenith of ethical leadership.

It signifies a commitment to values that transcend personal gain and speaks to the heart of what leadership should genuinely aspire to: service, integrity and an unwavering commitment to the greater good.

Why it is Hard to Tether Oneself to Noble Values

From the intoxication of authority, leaders may sometimes feel they tread on a plane beyond that of mere mortals, which leads them astray from their moral compasses. In a world that extols instant gratification, leaders face immense pressure to reap swift reward, sometimes at the expense of enduring, value-based outcomes. For a leader, vulnerability can be daunting. There is a pervasive belief that unwavering adherence to values might be construed as frailty, threatening their stature.

Amidst fierce competition, leaders may sometimes feel compelled to forsake the ethical high ground to maintain a vanguard position, seduced by the notion that victory can sanctify the means.

Ensconced within their circles of confidants, many risk becoming prisoners of homogenised thought. In such chambers of uniformity, deviation from noble values finds tacit endorsement. While under the pressure of momentous decisions, leaders may, at times, craft narratives of greater good to validate a corrupt course.

In a world where expedient actions reign supreme and sometimes over ethical deliberations, leaders may find themselves caught in the current, their values adrift.

Some may pursue an illustrious public persona over the authenticity of value-driven acts, leading to gestures that are a mere façade.

With every move under the magnifying glass, the dread of censure or failure can push leaders to paths that veer away from values, all in the quest to avoid the storm of public rebuke. Those who have curated an environment devoid of stringent checks and balances may feel an emboldening freedom, allowing them to disregard the ethical course.

Leadership is replete with varied tones. Many, through time, have chosen to walk the path of righteousness, often braving personal and professional tempests, while numerous more have failed to tether themselves to nobility.

Decision Checkpoints

In pursuit of tethering oneself to noble values, leaders should normalise asking these decision checkpoint questions

Integrity and authenticity

Am I making this decision based on the right thing to do, or am I being influenced by external pressures or personal gain?

Empathy and impact

How will this decision affect the well-being of all impacted, both in the immediate and long-term context?

Accountability and transparency

If every detail of this decision-making process were to be made public, would I still be proud and confident in my choice?

Resilience to temptation

Am I choosing the easier path or the right path? If faced with temptations or shortcuts, does this decision reflect my highest ethical standards?

Leading Beyond Now impact

How does this decision align with the legacy I want to leave, and how will it shape the future direction of the organisation or community I serve?

In the respected history of leadership, commitment is key to maintaining unwavering self-esteem, deep empathy and a strong, incorruptible spirit. However, leaders often find themselves tangled in the demands of society and their own desires, standing at the edge, wrestling with the strain of possibly going against their basic principles.

To rise above these complex challenges, leaders must hold onto values that are greater than their fleeting lives. They need to infuse empathy into every choice they make and uphold the importance of being incorruptible, pushing personal gain aside.
Our lives are filled with contrasts.

Every person seeks balance between light and dark, selflessness and selfishness, the temporary and the enduring. This delicate balance of opposites is natural and deeply crucial to leadership.

PART THREE
The Synergy of the
Five Commitments

Understanding each commitment independently is only the beginning of a transformative leadership journey. The true magic lies in realising how these commitments are interconnected and mutually reinforcing, creating a synergistic effect that amplifies the impact of each one.

A deep understanding of oneself is the starting point for all other commitments. When a leader is self-aware, they are more open to continuous learning, better attuned to empathise, more genuine in their authenticity, and can empower others more effectively.

By continually learning, leaders not only gain knowledge but also insights into human behaviour and perspectives. This makes it easier for them to empathise with others.

When leaders understand and connect with others on a deeper level, it becomes easier for them to be authentic. They no longer feel the need to put on a facade because they appreciate the value of genuine connection.

Those who prioritise integrity will naturally lean towards learning the truth and understanding others. Integrity ensures that knowledge is used ethically and that empathy is not feigned.

Supporting others as they seek to empower themselves is the natural result of a leader who understands themselves, continuously learns, connects with others authentically and acts with integrity.

The power of compounding

The principle of compounding is generally recognised in the financial realm, were small, consistent actions or investments over time lead to significant results, far exceeding the sum of individual actions. It is akin to a stone rolling down a hill, gathering momentum with each turn, becoming a formidable force by the time it reaches the bottom.

To illustrate, if you were to improve a skill by just one per cent every day, it may not seem like much daily, but over a year, the cumulative effect is that your skill would have improved by a staggering 37 times! It's not just the additive one per cent that matters, but the synergistic enhancement that this one per cent brings each day as it builds on the previous gains.

This compounding principle can be used with the Five Commitments by incorporating these practices.

Compounding self-awareness

Regular reflection and enhancement in self-awareness lead to better decision-making, more profound relationships and increased emotional intelligence, ultimately creating a more authentic and resonant leadership practice over time.

Compounding continuous learning

By dedicating time daily to learning, the acquired knowledge and skills amass and interact synergistically, making one a more versatile, informed, and effective leader, capable of adapting to various situations and challenges.

Compounding empathy

Consistent empathetic interactions cultivate deeper connections and mutual respect. Over time, this leads to heightened team morale and collaboration, fostering an environment where individuals feel valued and understood, enhancing overall productivity and innovation.

Compounding integrity

Regular acts of integrity strengthen one's moral compass and build an unassailable reputation of reliability and honesty. This cumulative trust and respect eventually translate into a harmonious and ethically sound way of leading.

Compounding empowerment and delegation

By routinely supporting empowerment and delegating, a leader nurtures autonomy and responsibility. The cumulative effect is a self-sufficient, highly motivated team, unlocking unprecedented levels of efficiency and innovation.

By making and reaffirming the Five Commitments, leaders do not merely add to their proficiency, but, rather, multiply their impact. The compounded synergies between Becoming a Worthy Custodian, Being Responsible with Influence, Curating Wise Counsel, Being Curious and Tethering Oneself to Noble Values; weave together to form a leadership ethic that is rich, diverse, and enduring.

This compounded impact does not just enhance the leader's journey; it elevates everyone around them, creating a ripple effect that can refine society and transcend conventional leadership paradigms. Envision throwing five stones into a pond. Each stone creates its ripple, but soon, the ripples intersect and amplify one another, creating a pattern more intricate and beautiful than any single ripple could achieve.

Cultivate synergy

Instead of isolating each commitment in your goal setting, look for goals that encompass two or more commitments, emphasising their interconnected nature.

In the vast, tumultuous seas of leadership, the winds of change blow unpredictably, and tides of challenges rise and fall. To stay committed is to embrace resilience, to brave the storm, knowing that the calm clarity of purpose lies beyond.

Every leader, no matter how steadfast, has faced the daunting shadows of doubt. These shadows question our worth, our decisions, and our path. They are the whispering voices that ask, 'Am I enough?'

It is not the absence of doubt but the courage to face it head-on that makes a leader. By admitting to our doubts and fears, we take the first step towards dispelling them.

Setbacks are not roadblocks, but intricacies waiting to be navigated. Each twist and turn, though perplexing, offers a lesson, an insight, an opportunity.

Instead of viewing setbacks as failures, see them as feedback. They are a way of saying, 'There's another way. Find it'.

With leadership comes the weight of expectation — both our own and those of others. This weight can be crushing, or it can be the force that grounds us, reminding us of our purpose.

While external expectations offer guidance, a leader's true north is their internal compass, crafted from their core values and vision. This compass ensures we stay true to ourselves, even in the face of mounting pressures.

Perfection is a mirage, ever elusive and misleading. The pursuit of perfection can lead us astray, making us lose sight of the essence of leadership: growth.

True leadership lies in embracing our imperfections, understanding that they're the scars of battles won, lessons learned, and growth achieved. Even in the darkest nights, the flame of commitment can be a beacon, guiding us back to our path.

The sapience of the Five Commitments is not merely in their individual significance, but in the harmony they create together. A leader who embodies all five does not just progress linearly; they evolve exponentially, *leading beyond now*.

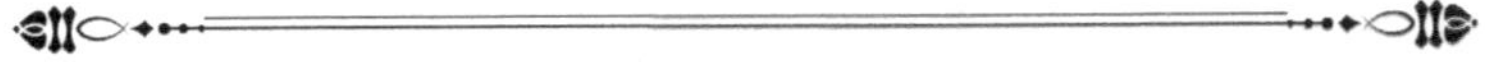

Acknowledgements

Who do you thank when you have written a work that is resultant from the entirety of your life experience? When the thing you have created is born from what you gained and what you lost? The list of people to acknowledge is inexhaustible, I focused therefore on those who shape me with their support and guidance.

My mother for being the embodiment of antifragility and love. My sister Chipo for being both the anchor and the sail for my dreams. My brothers, for always having my back.

My own Counsel of the Wise, the women who have and continue to shape, strengthen, and give my life vivacity - Natasha, Otsetswe, Gail, Mukami and Joy (also my insightful editor). Thank you for your love, humour, wisdom, and candour.

About the Author

Ethel Kuuya built a career in strategy, culture, leadership, transformation, public institution reform, policy-shaping, and senior leadership coaching. She engages in spirited dialogue with executives, national leaders, and think tanks, and setting the stage for transformational discussion.

Some of Ethel's achievements and recognitions include: 2018 Emerging New Leader Award by the Crans Montana Forum, a Swiss International Organisation; UNESCO Inclusive Policy Lab Expert; Chatham House Royal Institute for International Affairs forum contributor; former UN Women Civil Advisory Group Member; Non-Executive Director of various profit and not for profit organisations;

She has a Master of Science degree in Innovation and Entrepreneurship from HEC Paris, France which complements a portfolio of qualifications with various global institutions.

Ethel is a Zimbabwean who lives in the diaspora and works across Africa and internationally.

Resources

Find out more about:
- The Leading Beyond Now Coaching Programme
- Booking Ethel
- Private mentoring
- Advisory

www.ethelkuuya.com